samir mezrahi

milk and twitter: a selection of great tweets

milk and twitter: a selection of great tweets

illustrations by Larry Quach

First Edition, 2017

Kale Salad Inc

kalesalad.com

© Kale Salad 2017

ISBN 978-0692987414

Printed and bound in the United States

This book is dedicated to all of the people who lived before 280.

A special thanks to all of the creators who gave me permission to use their great tweets for this work as well as to all of the creators who make twitter the special place that it is every day.

first of all,

me: goodnight moon :)
moon: night<3
me: goodnight stars :)
moon: wtf
me: sry wrongnumber
moon: whos stars
moon: who is stars
moon: answer me

@jonnysun

socrates: i am wiser than this man; he
fancies he knows something, although he
knows nothing—
darryl, socrates' friend: fuck him up
socrates

@leyawn

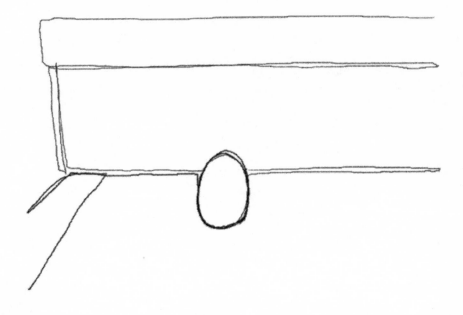

well, well, well, if it isn't the guy from twitter
that told me to go fuck myself

@dearjhonletter

so today i was lookin at a girl bcuz she had a
piece of lettuce in her hair & she looks at me
and said "i have a boyfriend" ok lettuce head

@bentono10

"sir, can i ask why you're smoking two huge
blunts?"
"officer, i'm..."
turns to camera
"double jointed"
cop starts breakdancing

@fred_delicious

if i pay $40 for a haunted house i better die

@hodgesboi

being 28-2016: i'm not ready for a
relationship
28-1816: i have 13 kids
28-1000bc: i lived a good life, thrice i ate a
berry and once a pear

@shutupmikeginn

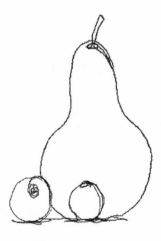

boy do i love sex. really love putting my
penis into some *looks at smudged writing
on hand* verguba

@sortabad

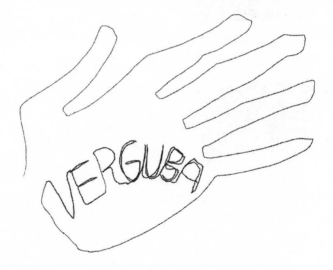

friend: how are things?

me: things are good!

narrator: things were not good

@keelyflaherty

hi, grandma? can u come pick me up from
my rap battle? it's over. no, i lost. he saw u
drop me off & did a pretty devastating rhyme
about it

@ch000ch

[sees girl reading the catcher in the rye]
"ah i love that book. The way he just
[clenches fist] catches all that frickin rye."

@david8hughes

just made some cornbread, bone app the
teeth

@godlytheruler

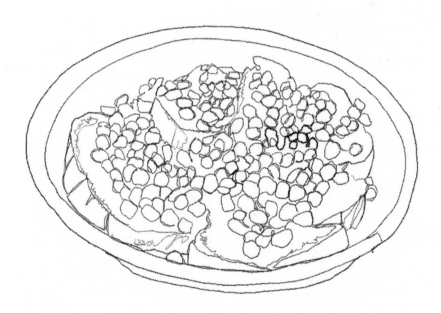

leaving my browser history open in case
anyone in this coffee shop tries to steal my
laptop when i'm in the bathroom.

@chelsea_elle

chrome.c//history

Admin Dictionary.com Facebook Twitter

History

Today - Sunday, March 16, 2014

12:55 PM WHY CAN NO ONE EVER HIDE FROM ME - Google Search www.google.com

12:53 PM CHELSEA LOCKWOOD WORLD FAMOUS KILLER - Google Search www.google.com

12:51 PM WHY WAS I BORN SO GOOD AT GUNS - Google Search www.google.com

12:51 PM WHY CAN I SMELL FEAR - Google Search www.google.com

12:47 PM BOBCATS WORLDS MOST EFFICIENT KILLERS - Google Search www.google.com

12:46 PM IS MY CAT A BOBCAT YES IT IS - Google Search www.google.com

12:45 PM WHY DO I LOVE TO FIGHT PEOPLE SO MUCH - Google Search www.google.com

12:44 PM WHY AM I NOT AFRAID OF MURDERING THIEVES - Google Search www.google.com

12:44 PM WHY AM I NOT AFRAID OF DEATH - Google Search www.google.com

12:42 PM Facebook www.facebook.com

12:42 PM WHY AM I SO GOOD AT GUNS - Google Search www.google.com

12:41 PM WHY AM I SO GOOD AT GUNS - Google Search www.google.com

12:40 PM AM I THE BEST STREET FIGHTER IN THE WORLD - Google Search www.google.com

shipwrecked diary
day 1: alone, doing well. mentally sound.
met a crab
day 2: i have married the crab.
day 3: i have eaten my wife.

@murrman5

[burglar gently waking me] you live like this?

@ericsshadow

record scratch

freeze frame

yup, that's me. you're probably wondering
how i ended up in this situation.

@a7xweeman

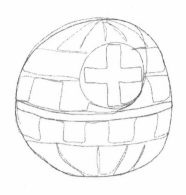

building inspector: what's this called
darth vader: the death—
[inspector's eyes look up from his clipboard]
darth vader: uh the health star

@bobvulfov

saw a pigeon having a job interview earlier. i
hope he got it.

@jamster83

milk and twitter

72938900R00017

Made in the USA
Lexington, KY
04 December 2017